"Children will sympathize with Gladys as her plans are repeatedly denied, changed, and frustrated by circumstances beyond her control. And they will rejoice as Gladys experiences the best plan of all: God's. In the pages of this book, young readers will be encouraged to attempt big things and then to trust God with the results."

MEGAN HILL, Editor, The Gospel Coalition; mother of four

"Will failing an exam keep Gladys Aylward from going to China? No! Laura Caputo-Wickham shows our kids how God makes a way for those he calls."

BARBARA REAOCH, Author, *A Jesus Christmas* and *A Better Than Anything Christmas*

"Gladys's story impacted me deeply. She was so willing, so hardworking, determined to overcome every barrier in her way to obey God's call to mission. The tremendous good she did for so many, at such great cost to herself, powerfully demonstrates what it looks like to follow in Christ's footsteps."

LINDA ALLCOCK, Author, *Head, Heart, Hands* and *Deeper Still*

"This is the amazing journey of a woman who never gave up, and whose faith in God took her all the way to China."

BOB HARTMAN, Author, *The Prisoners, the Earthquake and the Midnight Song*

"The wonderful storytelling and charming illustrations make the mini-biographies in this series pitch-perfect for even the youngest readers."

CHAMP THORNTON, Author, *The Radical Book for Kids*

"A wonderful series, beautifully illustrated, introducing your children to godly women."

BLAIR LINNE, Spoken Word Artist

Gladys Aylward

© Laura Caputo-Wickham / The Good Book Company 2021. Reprinted 2021.

Illustrated by Jessica Rose | Design and Art Direction by André Parker

"The Good Book For Children" is an imprint of The Good Book Company Ltd

thegoodbook.com | thegoodbook.co.uk | thegoodbook.com.au

thegoodbook.co.nz | thegoodbook.co.in

ISBN: 9781784986551 | Printed in Turkey

Do Great Things for God

Gladys Aylward

The Little Woman With a Big Dream

Laura Caputo-Wickham

Illustrated by Jess Rose

In cold, foggy London lived Gladys.

A little woman with a big dream.

Gladys longed to go to China.

At missionary school, she tried her best...

... but it didn't seem to be enough.

"Sorry Gladys," said her teacher,

"but you can't go to China".

Gladys had never been that
sad before.

One day, Gladys heard about Jeannie, an elderly missionary in China who needed help.

"I'll go!" offered Gladys.

But a train ticket to China was expensive, and all Gladys had were a few coins.

She sighed and put them on top of her Bible.

"Oh God," she prayed, "here's my Bible!
Here's my money! Here's me! Use me, God!"

Gladys worked hard every day and saved
all her money until she had enough...

... for a train ticket to China!

But the journey wasn't easy. Her train stopped in Siberia and wouldn't go any further.

Gladys had to cross a dark forest,
surrounded by packs of hungry wolves.

She met scary people who thought
she was a spy.

She sneaked onto a ship that
took her to Japan.

"Shhhhh."

She then took another boat...
another train...
a bus...

… and lastly a donkey!

Once in China, Gladys helped Jeannie.

The villagers, though, didn't trust her and threw mud at her!

Then the women had an idea:
"Let's open a guesthouse!"

And, just like that, the *"Inn of the Eighth Happiness"* opened its doors.

Tired travellers came in to get warm food and rest. And every evening, they listened to amazing stories from the Bible.

One day, the mandarin, a very important man, went to see Gladys.

He had a job for her.

"People are binding little girls' feet to keep them small," he said.

"They think it looks pretty, but it's very bad for them. Please, will you tell them to stop?"

Gladys accepted.

As she visited each village, she also told everyone about Jesus and how they could trust him as their King.

Little by little, the villagers began to trust Gladys and named her **Ai-weh-deh**, which meant "wise one".

AI-WEH-DEH

Gladys helped the poor and looked after the children who didn't have a family.

One day, she even stopped a nasty fight in a prison.
Angry men were kicking and punching.

"STOP!" shouted Gladys, and they all did at once!

Then, one day, scary aeroplanes flew over the mountains, dropping bombs on every village.

War had arrived.

When she saw how scared everyone was,
Gladys opened her Bible and read aloud:

*"Do not let your hearts be troubled.
Believe in God."* John 14 v 1

Gladys had to take 100 children to a safer village. They walked for days, until a deep river blocked their way.

There was no escape.

The enemy was coming to get them.

"Let's pray, Ai-weh-deh," said the children.

So, they asked God for help and they sang,

until...

… a boat came out of nowhere and took them to safety.

It was in moments like these that Gladys remembered just how safe she was with God, and that though she was only a little woman, her God was very, very BIG.

Gladys Aylward

1902 Gladys was the daughter of Rosina and Thomas Aylward. They lived in north London, where they led a simple but happy life.

While Gladys was attending church in her twenties, she felt called to serve God in China.

Determined to follow her dream, Gladys enrolled at missionary school.

Sadly, she didn't pass her theology exam and was told that she couldn't go to China after all.

But Gladys knew in her heart that she had to go. When she heard that Jeannie Lawson, an elderly missionary in China, needed a young woman to help her, Gladys offered to go. Jeannie agreed, provided that Gladys would pay for her journey there.

Gladys worked as a housemaid and picked up any extra job that she could find: sewing, waitressing, cleaning and more. And every penny she got she would put towards her train ticket.

1932 On October 15th Gladys packed two suitcases—one for her clothes and the other for tins of food, biscuits, tea, coffee and hard-boiled eggs. She also had a saucepan and a kettle tied to the bag. With a big smile on her face, she boarded the train.

After a long and rather scary journey involving trains, ships, wolves and angry men, Gladys arrived in China.

Though she wasn't welcome at first, with time Gladys earned the trust of those around her. She helped Jeannie to run a guesthouse for tired travellers, where they would read them stories from the Bible every night.

The mandarin, a very important man, became one of Gladys's best friends, and he offered her a job as "foot inspector". The Chinese emperor wanted to put an end to the tradition of binding little girls' feet in order to keep them small. Gladys was happy to help.

1938 When the Japanese attacked China, Gladys worked very hard at keeping people safe. Her faith in God helped her on many occasions when it looked as if there was no hope.

Gladys adopted a few children and opened an orphanage—a home for children with no family. She looked after 200 of them!

1949 Life in China had become very dangerous for Gladys, and she had to go back to England. But her heart was still beating for China, so, in her late fifties, she travelled to the island of Taiwan, where she opened another orphanage. She worked there until she died in 1970.

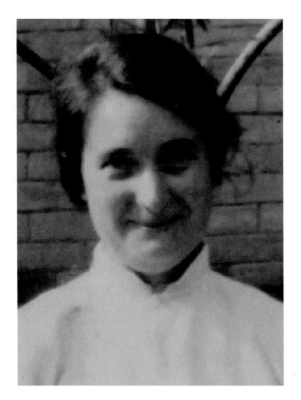

Gladys Aylward

1902 – 1970

"Do not let your hearts be troubled. Believe in God."

John 14 v 1

Do Great Things for God

Inspiring biographies for young children

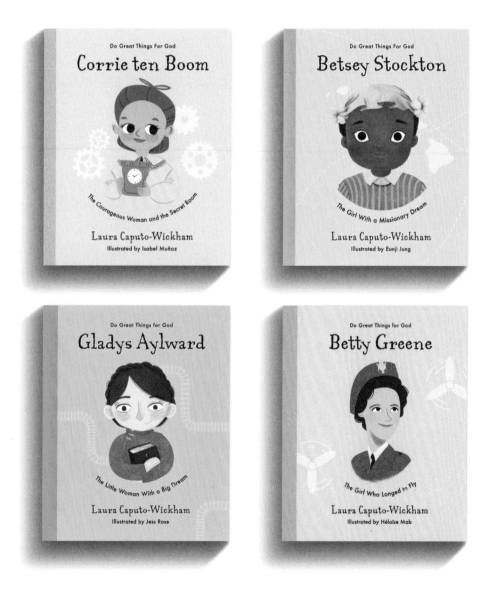